SEEING THE INVISIBLE GOD

Studies in the Gospel of John

CAROL BROWN

ECS
MINISTRIES
The Word to the World

Seeing the Invisible God

Carol Brown

Published by:
ECS Ministries
PO Box 1028
Dubuque, IA 52004-1028
phone: (563) 585-2070
email: ecsorders@ecsministries.org
website: www.ecsministries.org

First Edition 2013

ISBN 978-1-59387-192-5

SG-STIG

Printed in the United States of America

Contents

About the Gospel of John

John's gospel, written perhaps a generation later than the three Synoptic Gospels, is unique in its approach to the history of Jesus Christ's public ministry on earth. It is a highly artistic literary piece, not simply a chronicle of events. John, a Galilean fisherman who became a disciple of Jesus, has had time to reflect not just on what Jesus said and did but also on the significance of those words and actions. The earlier gospels attempted to provide a summary (synopsis) of Jesus' life and works; near the close of his book, John clearly states his rather different purpose:

> *Therefore many other signs Jesus also performed in the presence of the disciples, which are not written in this book; but these have been written so that you may believe that Jesus is the Christ, the Son of God; and that believing you may have life in His name. (John 20:30-31)*

Under the Holy Spirit's guidance, John selects from all the events he remembers those that contribute specifically to that purpose.

The gospel of John is a highly sophisticated literary narrative that includes specific, real settings, clear indications of time and geographical place. John's dramatic narrative style is characterized by much direct quotation of dialogue; he does not just tell the reader what was said, but allows us to hear the words as Jesus and others spoke them. We experience directly the grandeur of Jesus' claims to deity, the adoration of those who understood and believed, and the anger and outrage of the Jewish religious leaders of the day who set themselves in opposition to Him. Jesus Himself is, of course, the clear central character of John's account. Other characters that appear in the narrative are developed in relation to Jesus, always to the purpose of showing that Jesus is indeed the Christ, the Son of God.

The story is constructed with a clearly identifiable plot beginning with the prologue in the first eighteen verses of chapter 1. The rising action with its developing conflict begins with John the Baptist and continues to the climax of Jesus' crucifixion and resurrection. The plot's falling action (the resolution of the conflict) can be seen in Jesus' post-resurrection appearances, which John is careful to include as proof of the resurrection itself. The narrative's plot concludes with the epilogue of chapter 21 (parallel to the prologue of chapter 1), which defines the new situation, specifically the new relationship between Jesus and His disciples.

Although John tells the story from his own point of view, he does not use a first person ("I") viewpoint; instead, he uses third person pronouns ("he" or "they") in an effort to keep the focus always on Jesus. It is often the case that third person narrators are very unobtrusive, seeming to just disappear into the text. The reader of John's gospel, however, is always aware of John as narrator. John sometimes even interrupts the flow of the story to explain what he and the other disciples came to know or understand only afterwards (e.g. John 2:21-22; 6:71; 7:39; 13:11; 20:9) or to add a comment which explains or emphasizes a significance that the reader might otherwise miss (e.g. John 2:24-25; 6:64; 18:8-9).

About John, the Writer

Since the apostle John is the writer and it is from his point of view that we see Jesus in this gospel, it will be helpful to briefly consolidate what we know from Scripture about him.

John was probably a follower of John the Baptist before he met Jesus (John 1:35). His father was a Galilean fisherman named Zebedee. We know he had a brother, James. They seem to have had a family fishing business and to have worked closely with two brothers, Simon Peter and Andrew, from another fishing family (Matt. 4:21-22; Mark 1:16-20). One day Jesus called the four of them as John and James were in a boat mending nets. In their immediate response to Jesus' call, they simply left the nets they were mending and their father Zebedee. However, it appears that after some time spent with Jesus, the four went back to fishing, since there is another call of the four fishermen recorded in Luke 5:1-11. The call of Luke 5, accompanied by a miraculous catch of fish, seems to be the call to continuous service, since Jesus on that occasion told them, "From now on you will be catching men."

Jesus called John and James "Sons of Thunder" (Mark 3:17), perhaps because of their strong personalities. In one instance, John wanted to stop a man who was casting out demons because he was not part of Jesus' group of followers. Another time, when they came upon a Samaritan village that would not receive Jesus, James and John suggested calling down fire from heaven (Luke 9:49, 54). Some time later we see the mother of John and James looking out for her boys. Although it was she who asked Jesus if they might sit on His right and left when the kingdom comes, the sons themselves had clearly put her up to it (Matt. 20:21-22; Mark 10:35-45).

John was one of the "inner circle" of Jesus' disciples (the others being Peter and James). As such, he was one of the three who witnessed Jesus' transfiguration on the mount. John sat next to Jesus at the Last Supper and was with Him later that same night when Jesus was betrayed by Judas. It was John whom Jesus asked from the cross to take His mother Mary into his home.

After Jesus' resurrection and ascension, John was a pillar of the church at Jerusalem and a companion to Peter in the early spread of the gospel (Acts 3:1). He eventually moved to Ephesus (in Asia Minor, modern-day Turkey) and remained there until the Roman authorities exiled him to the island of Patmos.

Being one of the very first of Christ's disciples, John makes an excellent eyewitness and source of information about Jesus' entire public ministry, including the critical events of His crucifixion, resurrection, and bodily ascension back to heaven. John calls himself throughout his gospel by the self-effacing designation "the disciple that Jesus loved." By the time he wrote it, this was the feature of his relationship with Jesus that stood out to him as the most important.

In addition to this gospel, John wrote three letters that are preserved in Scripture (1, 2, 3 John) and also the Revelation. He lived to old age, perhaps until as late as AD 98.

ABOUT THIS STUDY GUIDE

As we have noted, John wrote his gospel so that people might believe that Jesus is indeed the Christ, the Son of God. However, in addition to its evangelistic purpose, the gospel of John has deep truth for those of us who have already believed.

The title of this series of studies, **Seeing the Invisible God,** is a reminder that in every lesson we are looking for what Jesus in His words and actions shows us about God, the One He came to reveal. Our God, who wants us to know Him and who remembers our limitations as earth-bound mortal beings, sent His Son to us as "the Word," the ultimate revelation of God to human beings:

> *No one has seen God at any time; the only begotten God who is in the bosom of the Father, He has explained Him. (John 1:18)*

That is why it is such a low moment when in chapter 14, just before Jesus is taken and crucified, Philip says, "Lord, show us the Father." Jesus answers, "Have I been so long with you, and yet you have not come to know Me, Philip? He who has seen Me has seen the Father; how can you say, 'Show us the Father'?"

The gospel of John is a lengthy book, one that would require many more lessons than this little study series can include. We have here ten lessons that specifically address who Jesus Himself said He is. They include, of course, the seven commonly identified "I am" statements that occur in John, as well as three other passages in which Jesus makes a particular identification of Himself using that "I am" construction. Those statements would seem to have a special relevance to our topic of "seeing the invisible God."

This study guide is intended for individual or group study. Most students will be able to study the passage in each lesson and write answers to the questions in about forty-five minutes to one hour. A discussion class time of about forty-five minutes once a week will enable students to share their answers and learn from one another. The discussion leader should feel free to select questions according to the needs of his or her group. You will find at the end of the study guide a section called **Leader's Notes** which contains additional material that the lesson leader may find helpful.

Most of the questions included in this guide are just study questions; they ask the student to read and think about the text. In order to keep our focus each week on "seeing the invisible God," there are a few additional questions at the end of each lesson under these three headings:

- "We wish to see Jesus" (from John 12:21)
- "Show us the Father" (from John 14:8)
- Personal Application

Like Philip, we do not have much excuse for thinking we cannot know the Father with the availability of this gospel, for it is the story of how His one and only Son walked on earth as the man Jesus Christ and explained and demonstrated to us the invisible God.

May God bless you as you study this precious gospel, and may we all truly, with the eyes of faith, see in its pages the invisible God.

STUDY ONE

John 1:1-18

THE WORD

John's gospel is the story of the things Jesus said and did that proved Him to be God in human flesh (20:30-31). Even though the main thrust of this series of lessons is a study of the "I am" statements that Jesus Christ made—the ways He defined and identified Himself as He was here on earth—it will be useful in this first lesson to establish the context in which those statements are reported. Thus we begin our study of the gospel of John with what is commonly known as the *prologue* to the book.

This opening passage gives us the information we need in order to understand the significance of the story John will tell. Specifically, we will not understand why the life, death, and resurrection of Jesus are so important if we do not realize that He is God. That truth (that Jesus is God) is the main thrust of these first eighteen verses of John. In addition, many of the key words and most of the major themes that we encounter later in the gospel are introduced here, like *life, light, darkness, believe, world,* and *witness.* John comes back again and again to these words and uses their repeated images and concepts to unify his gospel. Major themes that are introduced here and developed throughout the book include:

- Christ's deity and His oneness with the Father (vv. 1-3, 14, 18)
- Christ's rejection by the world and by His own people (vv. 10-11)
- Christ's acceptance by individuals (v. 12)
- Spiritual birth (vv. 12-13)
- Christ's glory and grace (vv. 14, 16-17)
- Christ's revelation of the Father (v. 18)

This prologue thus serves as an abstract—a brief encapsulation—of all that will follow, and gives us a concise context for Jesus' statements about Himself.

Begin your study by reading John 1:1-18.

1. Write down everything you learn about the Word from verses 1-3.

Goes back to Genesis where God created everything

2. Where are life and enlightenment to be found (v. 4)? What do you think these terms ("life" and "light") include (vv. 4, 9)?

That life came from God
Life was the light of all mankind.

3. What is the relationship between light and darkness in verse 5?

4. Who sent John (the Baptist), and why did he come (vv. 6-7)? What potential confusion about John is cleared up in verse 8?

God sent him to be a witness to testify concerning light, that all might believe
A witness

Indicates further information in the "Leader's Notes" section.

5. Verse 9 says that the Light came into the world. What were the responses to His coming (vv. 10-13)?

6. Verses 14-17 tell of the Word's incarnation (His coming in human form). How can you tell from these verses that the Word is Jesus Christ?

7. What do you learn about John the Baptist from his statement quoted in verse 15?

8. What contrasts do you see in verse 17 and why are they important?

9. Verse 18 gives us the reason that God the Son came to earth in the person of Jesus Christ. What was that reason?

"We wish to see Jesus."

10. List the names or titles used of Jesus in this passage.

11. What main truths about Jesus are presented here?

"Show us the Father."

12. What important things do you learn about God the Father from this passage?

PERSONAL APPLICATION

13. How has "the true Light" enlightened you?

14. What does it mean to you that Jesus Christ is called "the Word"?

15. How could John the Baptist's witness and testimony (vv. 6-8, 15) serve as an example for your life?

16. What changes will you make in your life based on your study of this passage?

As your lists above no doubt show, this opening passage of the gospel of John teaches us much about God the Father, about Jesus Christ, His Son, about the world and its opposition to God, and about the availability of salvation for all who will receive Christ. Although it is not stated directly, God's love for the world He created is strongly implied. Why else would He send His "only begotten" into the darkness to face opposition and rejection by His own creation? God's love for people is clearly the motivation for what we read here about Christ's coming to "explain" the God we cannot see. His love makes the offer to us of a place in His family, "the right to become children of God" through simple faith in His name.

We who have received Him, who have become His children, should bear a family resemblance to our Father. We should love the world that He loves, and we should show that love in what we do, just as God showed His love for the world by what *He* did—specifically, by sending His Son. Jesus came to bring grace and truth. These should characterize us as well. Grace should be evident in our gentleness, humility, and forgiveness. Truth shown in our integrity and faithfulness should be the hallmark of our dealings with others. Jesus came and "explained" the invisible God, but for people looking for a glimpse of Him today, the incarnation they may most readily see is His likeness in the life of a believer.

STUDY TWO

John 4:1-42

THE MESSIAH

In chapter 4 of his gospel, John presents the engaging story of Jesus' meeting with the Samaritan woman in Sychar at Jacob's well. John gives his account of this event in narrative form, allowing the reader to learn about Jesus' identity and character from what He says and does as He meets and talks to the woman who comes to draw water. John is at great pains to give very precise information about the setting of this little vignette as he provides the time and place of these events and the reason Jesus was there at all. These specifics powerfully testify to the veracity of his account and the reality of the events and conversations he records.

Here we find Jesus, as in chapter 3 with Nicodemus, engaged in a one-to-one conversation with someone who desperately needed what He had come to offer. The woman misunderstands Jesus' spiritual teaching at first, just as Nicodemus did, thinking He is talking of physical, literal things. In both cases, Jesus reveals new and important truths about Himself and the Father. Both the woman and Nicodemus learn through their encounters with Jesus that most of their thinking about God and spiritual realities is woefully inadequate, if not altogether mistaken.

Jesus left Judea to return to Galilee because the Jewish leaders were becoming very interested in what was going on out in the country where both John the Baptist and Jesus were preaching and baptizing. Jesus knew they had heard that His disciples were baptizing more people than John was, so it was likely that the focus of their hostility now included Jesus as well as John. Verse 4 tells us He had to pass through Samaria, a region most Jewish people would have avoided. He "had to," not because it was the only route geographically speaking, but because of His mission to a needy woman and the people of her town.

In this narrative, Jesus offers living water (v. 10), identifies Himself as the Messiah (v. 26), and is recognized as the Savior of the world (v. 42).

Begin your study by reading John 4:1-42.

1. What are the circumstances under which Jesus meets the Samaritan woman in Sychar (vv. 5-6)?

He went to Jacobs well in Samaria on His way to Galilee

2. Why is the woman so surprised when Jesus asks her for a drink (v. 9)?

Because she was a Samaritan

3. What is her personal history, and why is it important and relevant (vv. 16-18; 29)?

She said she had no husband, but Jesus knew she had had 5 husbands. Jesus knew she'd had ... Knew her history.

4. At what point in the conversation does she first understand that Jesus has been talking about spiritual water, not literal water?

5. Why do you think she introduces the subject of where one ought to worship God (v. 20)?

6. What does Jesus reveal to this woman about Himself (v. 26)? What effect does that revelation have on her?

John makes clear in verse 25 that the terms *Messiah* (Hebrew) and *Christ* (Greek) are equivalent in meaning. Both terms mean "anointed one." Those anointed in the Old Testament were usually kings or priests. The act of anointing was a symbolic recognition that a person had been called by God to a particular task or service. Think for a minute about what it means that Jesus came as the Messiah and that He was fully aware of it. In the simplest sense, He came to complete a task or service to which He had been appointed by God, that of redeeming sinners and reconciling them to God through His death on the cross. The fact that He was fully aware of why He had come and of who He was clearly testifies to His divine nature. That He was anointed for this task means that His death on the cross was not an accident or a martyrdom, but the fulfillment of the purpose for which He came. Of course, His role as the Son of David who will sit on David's throne forever awaits future fulfillment. His role as our Great High Priest and Advocate with the Father is ongoing now (Heb. 7:25-27).

7. In verses 31-38 Jesus speaks to His disciples. Do *they* recognize the spiritual significance of His words? Summarize briefly what He teaches them.

8. What is the effect of the Samaritan woman's story on the people of her town (vv.39-42)?

"WE WISH TO SEE JESUS"

9. The Samaritans recognized Jesus as "the Savior of the world" (v. 42). Why is that title so appropriate in this context? Look back at John 1:29 and 3:16-17.

10. In verses 6-7 John tells us that Jesus was "wearied from His journey" and that He asked for a drink. What do those facts reveal about His nature?

"Show us the Father"

11. What three great truths about God the Father does Jesus state in verses 23-24? What do each of those truths mean for your understanding of God?

Personal Application

12. If you have received Jesus' gift of living water, have you recently told anyone about what He has done for you? With whom will you next share the good news, and when?

13. How are you at work in the Lord's harvest? Where are you sowing and where are you reaping?

John 4 gives us the lovely story of Jesus' care and concern for a sinful woman and of her response to His revelation that He is indeed the Messiah, the anointed one sent from heaven as the Savior of the world. We note that faith results in action. It changes a life, and it affects others. The woman believes Jesus when He says He is the promised Messiah, leaves her everyday concerns with the well and the water pot, and goes immediately to the city to invite others to come and see for themselves. Though some believe because of the woman's testimony, others believe based on their own encounter with Jesus. The simple process presented here in narrative form illustrates clearly God's plan for bringing people to faith in Christ. As believers in Christ we share with others what He has done for us, but it is He who draws them to Himself and saves them, and thus their faith is in Him. That faith involves coming to know Christ Himself, not just the benefits He provides. We see at the outset of Jesus' conversation with the woman (v. 10) that the real issue is that she does not know who He is. She certainly needs the living water He can give, but that would follow almost as a matter of course if only she knew Him. Again there is a present-day application for us: we need to seek Him, to know Him, and to recognize that Jesus Christ Himself is the "gift of God."

How thankful we must be that Jesus, the Son of God, the Messiah, "had to" go through Samaria! He took the message that He is the Savior of the world to a sinful woman who, as a Samaritan, had no claim on Him and no special relationship with God. She was a woman of this world living for the things of this life. That is just where we all were before the intervention of the gospel of Christ in our lives, so it is easy for most of us to identify with her. Yet some people even today are outwardly more like Nicodemus in the previous chapter of John. He was a respected religious person, a Pharisee, who knew much about the Scriptures and enjoyed privilege and prestige in his society. The point John makes is that both of these people were important enough to Jesus to warrant a private talk in which He revealed majestic truths of who He is and what He gives: He is the Messiah, the Savior of the world, who offers new birth, living water, eternal life.

STUDY THREE

John 6:26-71

THE BREAD OF LIFE

John 6 brings us to the great discourse in which Jesus identifies Himself as the bread of life. It is the first of several metaphorical statements that Jesus uses to explain who He is. In later chapters we will encounter others such as "I am the Light of the world," "I am the door," "I am the good shepherd," and "I am the true vine."

This is a good opportunity to think for a moment about why the Lord chooses to explain Himself in this way. The basis for every metaphor is a figurative comparison between things that are unlike each other in a literal way, and here Jesus uses something physical and familiar (bread) to explain the spiritual and unfamiliar to His hearers. This metaphor, as metaphors always do, comes laden with a richness of suggestion and connotation that goes beyond what a literal statement can convey. Of course, Jesus means to say that He is as necessary to our spiritual life as daily food is to our physical life. But the metaphorical statement, "I am the bread of life," also conveys the comfort and satisfaction that knowing Christ offers. The Lord Jesus chooses the most expansive forms of language available to convey who He is and what He can mean in our lives, yet human language must ultimately be inadequate to explain the infinite. After all, that is why it was necessary for the Son of God, the Word, to become flesh (John 1:14, 18).

The events recorded in John 6 took place just before Passover (v. 4), so those listening to Jesus in the synagogue that day would have had their minds on Moses, the great leader and lawgiver, and on the events that Passover commemorates. They would have been thinking of the substitutionary sacrifice of the Passover lamb, the unleavened bread, the freedom from Egypt, and the manna in the wilderness. They had made the connection the day before between Moses and Jesus: both had taught from a mountain, and both had provided food for a multitude. The crowd had wanted to "take Him by force to make Him king" (vv. 14-15). They hoped Jesus would also, like Moses, be a leader who would free them from bondage—in their case, bondage to the Romans. Here in the synagogue He explains what the food supplied on the mountainside was really all about.

A simple outline may help us follow the flow of thought through this lengthy passage:

I. Food which endures (John 6:26-34)
II. The bread of life (6:35-50)
III. Eating His flesh and drinking His blood (6:51-59)
IV. Responses to a "difficult statement" (6:60-71)

With this context and perspective in mind, begin your study by reading John 6:26-34.

1. What is the "work of God" (v. 29)? Does a person do this work to *earn* eternal life? (See verse 27.)

To believe in Jesus

2. Why do the people ask for a sign? (v. 30). What is wrong with their reasoning? (See also verses 36 and 69.)

3. The day before, the crowd perceived Jesus as another Moses or "the Prophet" Moses had prophesied would come (v. 14). What does Jesus correct about their view of Moses and the manna (vv. 32-33)?

Continue your reading with John 6:35-50.

4. Jesus identifies Himself in verse 35 and again in verse 48 as "the bread of life." What does that phrase teach you about Jesus?

That if you trust in Him you will have eternal life.

5. In what sense do those who claim the promise Jesus gives in verse 35 experience its fulfillment (a) once for all and (b) in an ongoing way?

6. From where does Jesus state repeatedly that He has come (vv. 33, 38, 50, 51, 58)? Why does that make the Jews grumble (vv. 41-42)?

7. Who will Jesus "raise up on the last day"? How are they described in each of the following verses?

v. 39

The will of the Father is that none will be lost if they come to the Son.

v. 40

Everyone that believes in Him will have eternal life.

v. 44

No one can be raised up unless the Father draws them

v. 54

whoever eats my flesh & drinks my blood!

Continue reading John 6:51-59.

8. What does Jesus mean in verses 51-56 when He talks about eating His flesh and drinking His blood? (Think about the context of His statements thus far and remember that the Lord's Supper had not yet been instituted.)

Now finish your reading with John 6:60-71.

9. What were the responses to this teaching of Jesus?

vv. 60-61

Grumbling was a hard teaching

v. 66

vv. 68-69

"We wish to see Jesus."

10. What do you see about Jesus in this chapter that is especially meaningful to you?

11. Think for a minute about the title Peter gives to the Lord, "the Holy One of God." What does that title tell you about Jesus and His effect on those who heard His teachings?

"Show us the Father."

12. According to this passage, what is the Father's role in imparting eternal life to people? (vv. 38, 40, 44, 65)

PERSONAL APPLICATION

13. What kind of food are you working for—that which perishes or that which endures to eternal life?

14. How do you respond when the Lord reveals something to you that you find difficult or hard to accept?

15. How are you presently feeding on Jesus Christ, taking Him into your being?

Reading / Studying the Word.

The people who listened to Jesus that day in the synagogue in Capernaum were "put off" by His talk of eating His flesh and drinking His blood. However, the eating and drinking metaphor for taking something into one's mind or spirit is not really so odd, except that Jesus applied it to Himself. We use similar metaphors when we say we devour books, drink in lectures, swallow stories (or lies), ruminate on a matter, or eat our own words.

Jesus' words in this passage are clearly the language of sacrifice. His Jewish listeners would have been familiar with the idea of literally eating the flesh of a sacrifice; they ate the Passover lamb after all, as well as most of the Levitical sacrifices. But drinking His blood was an arresting and scandalous idea (Lev. 17:11). The blood of the sacrifice was for God, given for atonement for sin, and strictly forbidden for human consumption. It was poured out on the altar and sprinkled on the tabernacle's furnishings and servants for cleansing from sin (Heb. 9:22).

Jesus used this shocking metaphor to focus attention on a critical truth. Though foreshadowed by the animal sacrifices commanded in Leviticus, Jesus' sacrifice of Himself would be completely different. It would result in the once-for-all cleansing of the soul from sin. He says that we must *by believing* eat the bread of His flesh for eternal life, but we must also *by believing* drink His blood of atonement for the forgiveness of sins. Until this point in John's gospel, we have not seen Jesus teach very directly about His coming death. Perhaps that is why even His disciples found this discourse "a difficult statement" (v. 60).

There is a sense in which we appropriate by faith Christ's sacrifice once and for all. Jesus said, "I am the bread of life; he who comes to Me will not hunger" and "he who believes in Me will never thirst." The believer, in coming to Jesus Christ, will be satisfied not just for a while, but will never hunger or thirst again. However, there is another sense in which we feed daily on Jesus Christ, our Bread of Life. We believe and trust Him in each circumstance of our lives. We experience real satisfaction in Him when we consciously look to Him to sustain us with "the food which endures to eternal life."

STUDY FOUR

John 8:12-59

THE ETERNAL ONE

It was extremely difficult for the Jewish leaders of Jesus' day to accept that Jesus was the eternal Son of God, and it is certainly no easier for people of our own day and time. Those of Jesus' time rightly understood that His assertion of His eternality was an implied claim to deity. From a human standpoint it was, and still is, hard to understand how someone who is truly and fully man can also be eternal God. Yet that is exactly what the Scriptures teach.

In chapters 7 and 8 of John's gospel we see Jesus in Jerusalem for the Feast of Tabernacles, about six months before He was crucified. As we read these chapters we observe opposition building against Him and people divided in their opinions of who He is (7:12). We also see His complete awareness of the Father's purpose and timetable as He says, and as John reminds the reader repeatedly, "His hour had not yet come."

Our passage from John 8 records Jesus speaking with both believers and unbelievers in the temple court. His teaching and answers to the challenges of the Jewish leaders contain clear claims to deity, to eternality, and to oneness with the Father. He begins with the metaphorical statement, "I am the Light of the world" (8:12), but soon moves to the very direct "I am He" (8:24, 28), concluding the encounter with the unmistakable "before Abraham was born, I am" (8:58). The Jewish leaders at that point were so enraged by what they heard as blasphemy that "they picked up stones to throw at Him" (8:59) with the intention of stoning Him to death.

Begin your study by reading John 8:12-30.

1. Jesus says in verse 12 that He is "the Light of the world." What aspects of His character or work is He explaining through this statement? (Reread also John 1:3-9; 3:17-21 and look ahead to John 9:5.)

who believes in Jesus is in or received the light, non believers are in darkness

2. Why are these Pharisees unable (or unwilling) to accept Jesus' testimony (vv. 14-15)?

3. What does Jesus say it is necessary to believe in order to avoid dying in one's sins (v. 24)?

4. In verse 28 Jesus again says, "I am He." What is He saying about His relationship to the Father and the source of His message? (vv. 28-29)

Continue your reading with John 8:31-59.

5. In verse 30 we learn that "many came to believe in Him." How do those who believe become His true disciples, and how are they rewarded (vv. 31-32)?

6. In verse 33 those listening to Jesus challenge His promise of freedom. What is their objection, and how does Jesus answer it?

7. What does Jesus say in response to the Jews' assertion, "Abraham is our father" (vv. 39-41)?

8. Whom do these Jews next claim as their "father" (v. 41)? According to what Jesus teaches them in response to this claim, why can the claim not be true?

9. Why do they not understand what Jesus is saying (v. 43)?

10. As Jesus answers the first two challenges, He says, "You also do the things which you heard from your father" (v. 38) and "You are doing the deeds of your father" (v. 41). In verse 44, Jesus clearly identifies their father: "the devil." What two specific characteristics of the devil does Jesus mention, and how are they particularly related to this conversation?

11. In verse 51 Jesus promises that anyone who "keeps [His] word . . . will never see death." What does it mean to "keep [His] word"? What do you understand "death" to mean in this context?

12. The Jews point out that Abraham and all the prophets died (v. 53). Jesus answers that "Abraham rejoiced to see My day, and he saw it and was glad" (v. 56). In what way did this occur? (Consider Hebrews 11:8-10 as well as this passage.)

13. The final exchange between Jesus and these Jews occurs in verses 57-59 ending with Jesus' assertion, "Truly, truly, I say to you, before Abraham was born, I am." How do the Jews react, and why? (See also Leviticus 24:16.)

"WE WISH TO SEE JESUS."

14. Jesus says three times in this chapter "I am" (Greek: *ego eimi*) in verses 24, 28, and 58. (See also Exodus 3:13-14 and Isaiah 41:4). What do you learn specifically about Jesus' deity from each of these three verses?

"SHOW US THE FATHER."

15. What do you see in each of the following verses about the relationship between the Son and the Father?

v. 16

v. 19

v. 26

v. 29

v. 42

v. 54

v. 55

PERSONAL APPLICATION

16. Is it possible to "have the Light of life" through faith in Jesus Christ and still "walk in the darkness" (v. 12)? Are there areas of your life into which you need to let His light shine?

17. From what bondage has the truth of God's Word freed you (vv. 31-32)?

From a literary standpoint, we see in chapters 7 and 8 that John uses the increasing opposition to Jesus as the conflict which drives the plot's rising action. That conflict will reach its climax as Jesus is crucified (chapter 19). As early as chapter 5, John tells us "the Jews were seeking all the more to kill Him" (v. 18), a point he makes repeatedly in chapters 7 and 8 (7:1, 19, 25; 8:37, 40). Additionally, John's use of direct quotation in the dialogue in chapter 8 makes the emotional content of the Jews' anger and hatred immediate and real to us as readers.

These Jews are not challenging Jesus in a primarily intellectual way; neither their minds nor their hearts are open to what He teaches about Himself. Yet the importance and richness of John 8 lies in Jesus' revelation of His deity, His eternality, and His relationship with the Father. The details provided there "flesh out" John's summary statements of chapter 1 that "the Word was God" (v. 1) and "the only begotten God who is in the bosom of the Father, He has explained Him" (v. 18). In chapter 8, as Jesus talks with the Pharisees in the temple, He refers repeatedly to "the Father who sent [Him]." He clearly states that He speaks "as the Father taught [Him]," that He always does "the things that are pleasing to Him," and that the Father "has not left [Him] alone." Four times He identifies Himself as "I am" (vv. 12, 24, 28, and 58), the name by which Jehovah identified Himself to Moses at the burning bush. Jesus' call is to follow Him, to believe in Him, to find in Him not only how to gain eternal life, but knowledge of God Himself. He says in verse 19, "If you knew Me, you would know My Father also."

The Pharisees who were challenging Him that day in the temple clearly did not know Him and did not know the Father whom they claimed as their own (v. 41). The anger and animosity of the exchange recorded in chapter 8 underline the spiritual blindness of these who rejected "the Light of the world."

STUDY FIVE

John 9:1-41

THE LIGHT OF THE WORLD

As has often been noted, John records in his gospel only a carefully selected few of the miracles that Jesus performed in the three years of His public ministry. John always refers to these as *signs*. He wants the reader to realize that Jesus was not just a miracle worker or a spiritually empowered prophet, but the true Son of God, and that *the purpose of the signs was to authenticate His claim to deity*. The signs reveal not just His divine power, but also His holy character.

The signs are often linked to Jesus' own teaching about who He is. Here in chapter 9, He says once again that He is "the Light of the world" (v. 5), just as is recorded in John 8:12. At first glance, the contexts of these two chapters seem to be very different, and it may be hard to understand what this statement, "I am the Light of the world," really signifies. In chapter 8, Jesus speaks of Himself as the Light of true discernment and judgment of sin (vv. 15-16, 23-26). In chapter 9, the Light is linked to both physical and spiritual vision through the sign of the healing of the man born blind. In both cases the Light of the world is seen in contrast to the darkness of sin and the blindness it causes. It is easy to apply the truths of these chapters to ourselves, for surely we are all born blind spiritually as a result of sin, and we all need the healing miracle that only the Light of the world can bestow—to have our eyes opened, our blindness healed, and the darkness of sin dispelled. Only after we experience the mercy of His healing and cleansing by exercising faith in Christ will we able to face the searching light of His righteous judgment (9:39).

The wonderful account of the healing of the man born blind in chapter 9 of John's gospel is given in very vivid and memorable form. It is a highly dramatic little vignette containing characters with real personality, lots of intense conflict, and emotional dialogue. We understand the fear of the man's parents before the haughty and intimidating Pharisees and the increasing frustration and sarcasm of the healed man as he is questioned repeatedly. We are touched by the compassion and kindness of the Lord Jesus, who sees at the beginning of the story the blind beggar whom no one else seems to notice, and who at the conclusion seeks out the man who has been expelled from the synagogue. Through scenes such as this one, we as readers understand the depth of emotion that Jesus aroused. We observe the simple faith of a healed blind man set against the rage of the Pharisees, who were witnessing their carefully constructed world being upended.

Begin your study by reading John 9:1-41.

1. What does the question of verse 2 reveal about the disciples' view of sin and human suffering? What does Jesus teach about these subjects in verse 3?

2. In verse 5 Jesus says, "While I am in the world, I am the Light of the world." Is He *still* in the world? Is He *still* the Light of the world? (See Matthew 5:14 and Ephesians 5:8-14.)

3. How does the blind man demonstrate his faith in Jesus (v. 7)?

4. How do the following people react to this display of the "works of God"?

a. the neighbors (vv. 8-12)

b. the Pharisees (vv. 15-18; 28-29; 34)

c. the man's parents (vv. 20-23)

d. the man himself (vv. 30-33)

5. How does the formerly blind man receive *spiritual* sight (vv. 35-38)?

6. In verses 39-41, who are "those who do not see," and who are "those who see"?

"WE WISH TO SEE JESUS."

7. In verse 5, Jesus repeats His statement of 8:12, "I am the Light of the world." How does this sign (the healing of the man born blind) illustrate His statement?

8. From this chapter, what examples do you see of Jesus' grace, love, and compassion in both His words and deeds?

"SHOW US THE FATHER."

9. From verses 3-4, what are the "works of God"? How can we recognize the "works of God" in our world today?

10. Read 1 John 1:5. How does Jesus' statement, "I am the Light of the world," particularly reveal to us the invisible God?

PERSONAL APPLICATION

11. In a spiritual sense we all have been born blind. How has the Lord opened your eyes spiritually?

12. Can you think of trials or troubles you have suffered that you believe came into your life "that the works of God might be displayed in [you]"? Why do you think we are so quick to attribute all our suffering to personal sin? How should the Lord's teaching in John 9:3 affect our view of other people's suffering?

13. The formerly blind man faced the opposition of the Pharisees alone. Not even his parents stood with him. How can you stand with and support those who are suffering for their faith in Christ?

Let's take a moment to notice how this healed man's understanding grew as he responded in faith to each revelation God gave him. Immediately after his healing, the neighbors who had known him as the blind beggar asked what had happened. As the man answers he refers to Jesus simply as "the man they call Jesus" (v. 11). A little later, as the Pharisees ask for his analysis of who Jesus is, the healed man says, "He is a prophet" (v. 17). As the discussion about his healing becomes more heated, the man's reasoned conclusion becomes, "If this man were not from God, He could do nothing" (v. 33). Finally, after he is put out of the synagogue, Jesus comes to him and asks him directly, "Do you believe in the Son of Man?" The man answers, "Lord, I believe" and worships Him (v. 38). He has recognized Jesus as God. We notice that he worships only when he understands who Jesus is. This worship was not about what Jesus had done for him; what Jesus did in healing him was the sign that led him to the truth of who Jesus is. The man does not worship even a miracle-performing prophet (nor should he). Only the recognition that Jesus is God leads him to worship.

As we conclude our study of this wonderful sign, let's ask the Holy Spirit to help us to respond in faith by worshipping Christ and bearing a clear testimony to others of what we know of the Lord. Then He will surely reveal more and more of Himself as we act on the revelation we have. In the words of Charles Spurgeon:

If now with eyes defiled and dim,
We see the signs, but see not Him;
O, may His love the scales displace,
And bid us see Him face to face.

S T U D Y S I X

John 10:1-30

THE GOOD SHEPHERD

Jesus' teaching in John 10 is presented in a form completely different from the dramatic narrative of chapter 9. Here Jesus uses an analogy in which He speaks of Himself and those who follow Him in terms of a shepherd and his sheep.

For the people of the Middle East in Jesus' time the picture would have been clear; for twenty-first century urban Americans it may not be. Briefly then, the *fold*, or sheep pen, was a large walled or fenced enclosure in which the sheep were left at night for protection from predators and to keep them from wandering off. Sometimes several shepherds grazing their sheep in the same area left their flocks together in this large fold. The enclosure had one opening (or door) which the doorkeeper guarded through the night. In the morning, each shepherd came to the door and called his sheep. The sheep, recognizing their own shepherd's voice, would follow him out of the fold to the fields where they would graze that day.

In the analogy, Jesus is, of course, the shepherd, and believers (His followers) are the sheep.

Begin your study by reading John 10:1-30.

1. Jesus tells the story of the shepherd and sheep in verses 1-5. To whom is He addressing this story? (Look back to the end of chapter 9.) Do they understand what He is saying?

2. Jesus says in verses 7 and 9, "I am the door." What is He teaching about Himself through this statement?

3. Who might the thieves and robbers be (vv. 1, 8, 10)? What do they do? Note the contrast in verse 10 to what Jesus, the good shepherd, does.

4. Jesus says in verses 11 and 14, "I am the good shepherd." In verse 11 what specifically makes Him the *good* shepherd?

5. What characterizes the hired hand of verse 12? How is the hired hand contrasted to the good shepherd? Who do you think are the hired hands that Jesus speaks of here?

6. Who are the "other sheep" of verse 16?

7. Jesus speaks at least 5 times in this short passage of "laying down" His life for the sheep (vv. 11, 15, 17-18). Why is this wording so important?

8. Why do these Jewish leaders gathered around Jesus in Solomon's Porch at the Feast of the Dedication not believe (v. 26)?

9. John 10:27-30 teaches what great truth about those who are the sheep of the Good Shepherd?

"WE WISH TO SEE JESUS"

10. In this chapter we see the Lord Jesus Christ as the Good Shepherd. Look up Hebrews 13: 20-21 and 1 Peter 5:4 to see two other ways He is described as a shepherd.

11. What attributes of Jesus' character are most clearly revealed as He speaks of Himself as the Good Shepherd?

"SHOW US THE FATHER"

12. In the Old Testament, Jehovah is often presented as the Shepherd of His people. Probably the best known passage is Psalm 23. Take a few minutes to read it, thinking of how Jesus, the Good Shepherd, shows us the Father. Write down your insights.

PERSONAL APPLICATION

13. Which verses from chapter 10 . . .

a. comfort you most?

b. make you most thankful?

c. cause you to worship the Lord?

The picture presented here in John 10 of the Good Shepherd and His sheep teaches great truths about the relationship of the Lord Jesus Christ with us who belong to Him. We are greatly comforted in knowing that He has called each of us by name, that He knows and loves each of us individually. We learn that our security in His flock rests entirely on His power to keep us, not our ability or determination to follow Him. We rest in His ability to protect and provide for us since He says, "I give eternal life to them, and they will never perish; and no one will snatch them out of My hand" (v. 28). The peace and security of the sheep rest ultimately in the power and ability of their shepherd. Verse 18 teaches us that our Good Shepherd has complete control and authority, even over His own death. He prophesies that He will lay down His life—no one can take it from Him—and then asserts His authority and power to take it again (v. 17).

STUDY SEVEN

John 11:1-46

THE RESURRECTION AND THE LIFE

Chapter 11 of John's gospel brings us to the seventh sign that John records; it is the final one except for Jesus' own resurrection. It is just before the raising of Lazarus that Jesus says to Martha, "I am the resurrection and the life." Several of the previous "I am" statements have been metaphorical, as when Jesus said, "I am the bread of life," "I am the Light of the world," "I am the door of the sheep," and "I am the good shepherd." This statement, "I am the resurrection and the life," is not metaphorical, but a quite direct literal statement of His authority over life and death. It takes the reader back to John 1:4, where John wrote, "In Him was life, and the life was the Light of men." It is of interest to note also that this statement is not made to a crowd but spoken personally to the grieving Martha as she has come out of the house to meet Jesus.

Again, as in John 9, we have a wonderfully engaging narrative in which John clearly delineates characters, reports much direct dialogue, and builds his account to a thrilling climax as Jesus calls Lazarus out of the tomb. Once again, the sign serves to illustrate the statement Jesus makes about His own identity.

Begin your study by reading John 11:1-46.

1. Do a little background reading on this family at Bethany in Luke 10:38-42, John 12:1-8, Matthew 26:6-13, and Mark 14:3-9. What do you learn about each member of the family?

Martha

Mary

Lazarus

2. What is the purpose of Lazarus's sickness and death (v. 4)? (Compare to John 9:3.)

3. What reasons does Jesus give for returning to Judea over the objections of the disciples (vv. 7-15)?

4. Jesus speaks of Lazarus's death as sleep. Look up these additional New Testament verses that use the word *sleep* in reference to a believer's death: Acts 7:60; 1 Corinthians 15:20; 1 Thessalonians 4:13-18. What does this word convey to you about the death of a believer in the Lord Jesus Christ?

5. Martha says in verse 24 that she knows Lazarus will rise again "on the last day." What truth about Himself does Jesus want her to see as He says, "I am the resurrection and the life" (v. 25)?

"WE WISH TO SEE JESUS"

6. How is the resurrection of Jesus as recorded in John 20:1-10 different from the raising of Lazarus as recorded in this passage?

7. Which verses in this chapter show Jesus' genuine humanity?

8. Which verses show His authentic deity?

"SHOW US THE FATHER"

9. What does Jesus' prayer (vv. 41-42) reveal about His relationship with the Father?

Personal Application

10. The sisters send word of the situation with Lazarus in verse 3; verse 5 tells us that Jesus loved all three of these people; and, verse 6 tells us that Jesus waited two more days before beginning His journey to Bethany. What could you learn from these verses that might help you the next time the Lord seems to delay in answering your prayers?

11. What is the value of public, audible prayer (see verses 41-42)?

12. What does it mean to you personally that Jesus Christ is the resurrection and the life?

Once again, John records for us the divided response of the people to a dramatic sign, the most dramatic one up until now. Many of the Jews who have come from Jerusalem to comfort Mary (and Martha) and to mourn the death of Lazarus believe in Jesus because of what they witness (v. 45). Others, though, go back to the

Pharisees and report what Jesus has done (v. 46), presumably with no good in mind. The final verses of chapter 11 record a meeting of the Sanhedrin in which the priests and leaders of the Jewish nation pledge themselves to bringing about Jesus' death. It is interesting to note that these unbelieving Jews do not dispute the authenticity of the signs, but they refuse to accept the truth to which they point—that Jesus is indeed the Christ, the Son of God, just as He says He is. It seems highly ironic that the raising of Lazarus sets in motion the events that lead directly to the death of Jesus. One last time, Jesus withdraws with His disciples to the city of Ephraim (v. 54). Passover will take place soon, when He will die as the Passover sacrifice, the Lamb of God.

STUDY EIGHT

John 14:1-31

THE WAY, THE TRUTH, AND THE LIFE

"Do not let your hearts be troubled" (v. 1) are the comforting words that open John 14, and which close it as well (v. 27). Jesus is speaking in the upper room to His disciples after their final Passover meal together. He has washed their feet, and Judas has gone out to betray Him. Jesus spends these last hours before His crucifixion and death ministering to His faithful disciples. In this chapter, His primary objective seems to be to reassure and prepare His followers for what is about to happen (v. 29). The chapter may be divided into four sections, each of which explains a truth that will comfort the disciples and bolster their faith in the days and years ahead:

I. The promise of a home in heaven (vv.1-6)
II. The oneness of the Father and the Son (vv. 7-15)
III. The promise of the indwelling Holy Spirit (vv. 16-26)
IV. The gift of peace (vv. 27-31)

Begin your study by reading John 14:1-6.

1. In John 14, Jesus comforts His disciples. What have they recently learned that would have troubled and discouraged them?

John 12:23, 32-33

John 13:21

John 13:33, 36

John 13:38

Matthew 26:31

2. How does Jesus describe His Father's house (vv. 2-3)? For the disciples, what would be the most comforting information included in this description?

3. How does one get to the Father's house, heaven (v. 6)? Is there any other way?

4. Jesus says He is "the truth" (v. 6). What does that rather broad statement encompass? (See John 1:14, 17; 6:32-33, 55; 8:32; and 15:1.)

5. Explain what Jesus means when He says, "I am . . . the life" (v. 6). What more is He talking about than just life that never ends? Consider John 1:4; 3:16; 5:26; and 10:10.

Continue reading John 14:7-15.

6. What are Jesus' promises concerning prayer in verses 13-14? How are these promises related to the Son's oneness with the Father, the subject of verses 7-12?

7. How do believers show their love for the Lord (vv. 15, 21, 23)? How does Jesus show His love for the Father (v. 31)?

Now read John 14:16-31.

8. Who will the Father give to believers at Jesus' request (vv. 16-17)?

9. What truths about the Holy Spirit does Jesus teach in this chapter?

v. 16

v. 17

v. 26

10. What is Jesus' gift to the disciples (v. 27)? How is His giving "not as the world gives"?

"WE WISH TO SEE JESUS"

11. List at least three things from this chapter that Jesus does for every person who believes in Him, citing the verse in which it is mentioned.

"SHOW US THE FATHER"

12. List at least three things from this chapter that the Father does for each believer, citing the verse in which it is mentioned.

13. In what ways has Jesus already shown Philip the Father (vv. 7-11)?

PERSONAL APPLICATION

14. What are some truths from this chapter that could keep *your* heart from being troubled?

15. Now, think of something going on in your life right now that troubles your heart. How can you specifically apply your answers to questions 11 and 12 to that situation and allow the Lord Jesus to minister His peace to you?

Jesus' words of comfort must surely have helped His disciples that night, and they must surely help us in whatever unsettling circumstances we may find ourselves. The promises of answered prayer, the indwelling Holy Spirit, and a home in heaven as well as the gift of peace, though, entirely depend on the oneness of Jesus with the Father. That is the truth of this passage which is most essential to our comfort and peace. If Jesus were not one with the Father, none of these promises could have any meaning; it is only because Jesus is God that He is able to give them. Jesus tells Philip and the others, "He who has seen Me has seen the Father." Both His words and His works attest the truth of that statement. This precious passage shows us that Jesus is "the way, and the truth, and the life," and we come to the Father only through Him because He is the only one who has come down from the Father to us.

STUDY NINE

John 15:1-16

THE VINE

As we have already noticed, the later "I am" statements of Jesus that John records are not spoken to crowds of people or in public settings. Jesus is nearing the end of His time on earth, and His focus is on the small band of disciples that remain with Him, now only eleven in number. His purpose in this last evening together with them before His death is to reassure them that they will not be alone after He is gone, to comfort them in their grief, and to strengthen them to carry on the work without His physical presence. They have heard Him say "I am" (8:24, 28) and "before Abraham was born, I am" (8:58), asserting His deity and emphasizing His oneness with the Father. Jesus' statement here in John 15:1, "I am the true vine," and His identification of believers as branches, emphasize His oneness with them. It is a relationship so close and so essential to the life of the believer that Jesus plainly states, "Apart from Me you can do nothing" (v. 5). As we learn later in the chapter, this unity of Jesus with believers has as its pattern the oneness of the Father and Son (vv. 9-10). What an amazing thought it is that human beings can be brought into such closeness with the Son of God, and through Him with the Father!

Begin your study by reading John 15:1-16.

1. What does Jesus mean when He says He is "the *true* vine"? Read Psalm 80:8-13 and Isaiah 5:1-7.

2. Verses 3-5 describe the relationship of the believer to Christ in terms of the branch to the vine.

a. What should characterize the relationship?

b. What is the goal of this relationship?

3. Who is "the branch in [Him] that does not bear fruit" (v. 2)? You might consider the following verses as you formulate an answer: John 10:27-30; 1 Corinthians 11:30-32; John 6:66; John 13:21; 1 John 2:19.

4. What can the branch (the believer) do apart from Christ, the vine (v. 5)?

5. In verse 6, who is the person who "does not abide in [Him]"? Is this person the same as or someone different from "the branch in [Him] that does not bear fruit" in verse 2?

6. What do you see in each of the following verses about what it means to abide in the vine?

v. 7

v. 8

vv. 9-10

v. 11

7. What do you think is the fruit that the believer bears as he or she abides in Christ, the vine? Consider Galatians 5:22 as well as the verses here in John 15, especially verse 16.

8. What is the difference between a servant and a friend (v. 15)?

9. What will Jesus do and what has He done to show His love for believers (vv. 13, 15)?

10. What does He ask of His "friends" (v. 14)?

11. From verses 7 and 16, what do you learn about prayer? (Look again at John 14:13-14 and list all that Jesus has taught in these passages about prayer.)

"WE WISH TO SEE JESUS"

12. Think over all this passage teaches about Jesus Christ as the true vine. Which of His attributes do you think this metaphor is intended to emphasize?

"Show us the Father"

13. What does the role of "vinedresser" (husbandman, gardener) convey about the Father's relationship to the Son and to believers?

14. Look again at verse 8. How does our bearing fruit glorify the Father?

Personal Application

15. Examine your own relationship with the Lord in the light of this passage, then answer the following questions before Him.

a. Am I really abiding in Him through His word (v. 7), prayer (vv. 7, 16), and obedience to His commands (vv. 10, 14)?

b. Is there fruit for God in my life? More fruit? Much fruit? Fruit that remains?

c. Do I have the joy that is promised to those who abide in Him (v. 11)?

16. What does it mean for you personally that Christ is the vine and you are one of the branches?

Jesus chooses to describe His relationship with believers in terms of a vine and its branches. The metaphor itself conveys to us that His life flows through us and produces fruit for the Father in our lives. This statement, like all the other "I am" statements, is meant primarily to reveal who Jesus is. This one, though, prompts us to think about who *we* are in Him and what His purposes are for us. In terms of the metaphor, much of our thinking centers round what it means to abide and bear fruit. To summarize: abiding in Him is linked to commitment to His teaching (v. 7), the power of prayer (vv. 7, 16), and obedience to His commands (v. 10). The result of abiding in Him is that we bear fruit which glorifies the Father and gives evidence that we are truly His disciples (v. 8). In addition, Jesus promises His joy here (v. 11), just as He promised His perfect peace in chapter 14.

Judas the betrayer will soon return with the soldiers who will take Jesus away from these faithful eleven. Jesus leaves them with these reminders that He has chosen them not just to be His servants; they are His friends, since He has brought them into the intimacy of sharing with them "all things" that He had heard from His Father (v. 15). Our enjoyment of that intimacy is one of the blessings of abiding in Him.

STUDY TEN

John 18:1-11

THE ONE IN CONTROL

Chapter 18 returns the reader to the action of the story John is telling. Chapters 14–17 have been taken up with the Upper Room Discourse and Jesus' intercessory prayer on behalf of His disciples and ultimately all believers. Jesus has washed His disciples' feet and eaten the Passover with them. He has spoken at length to them of the coming Holy Spirit, His availability to them through prayer, and the importance of loving one another. The disciples have heard Him intercede for them in Gethsemane and pray about the coming ordeal of the cross that He is about to face. Meanwhile Judas, who left immediately after receiving the morsel from Jesus at dinner (13:30), has been given both Roman soldiers and the Jewish temple officers to capture Jesus. As they approach Jesus, He once again says, "*ego eimi*," "I am." On the surface it seems that Jesus is just identifying Himself to individuals who would likely not recognize Him at night by torchlight. However, their reaction seems to suggest overtones to His statement that go beyond simple identification.

Begin your study by reading John 18:1-11.

1. Why was it so easy for Judas to lead the soldiers and officers directly to Jesus (vv. 1-3)?

2. Would Jesus and the disciples have known the soldiers were coming? What does Jesus do, and what would the soldiers have been expecting Him to do (vv. 3-4)?

3. Who takes the initiative in this encounter (v. 4)? Why?

4. What happens when Jesus identifies Himself (v. 6)? To what do you attribute this response?

5. Look back at John 7:32 and 45-46 for a similar response. What happened then?

6. What is the condition Jesus places upon His going with the soldiers who have come to arrest Him (v. 8)? According to John, why does He set this condition?

7. What does Peter do? What do you learn about Peter from verses 10-11? (See Matthew 26:52-53 and Luke 22:51 for the outcome of this incident.)

8. What is the "cup" Jesus speaks of in verse 11? See also Matthew 20:22-23 and 26:39, 42.

"We wish to see Jesus"

9. List the details from verses 1-11 which show that it was Jesus rather than Judas and the soldiers who was in control.

10. Look back at John 6:15-25, another occasion Jesus identifies Himself with "*ego eimi*" (there translated, "It is I"). What does the miracle recorded there show about His control over all things?

11. Would you say that John 18:1-11 displays more prominently Jesus' humanity or His deity?

"SHOW US THE FATHER"

12. What does this incident reveal about the Father's attitude toward sinful men who are clearly at enmity with Him?

13. What does this encounter in Gethsemane reveal about the Father's faithfulness to believers in Christ?

PERSONAL APPLICATION

14. What lessons for your own life can you learn from Peter as you see him here and in verses 15-18 and 25-27 of this chapter?

15. How would it help you today to remember that God is in control of every detail of your life?

The event we have looked at in this lesson shows us Jesus' control over the entire situation of His arrest. A contingent of soldiers with torches and weapons would seem able to gain control over twelve men alone in a garden at night. However, as we read John's account we see very clearly that just as Jesus controlled the winds and the waves and the laws of physics when He walked on the Sea of Galilee, so Jesus controls all men whether or not they consciously yield control to Him. These soldiers are powerless to take Him unless He allows it (8:59). Once again John offers an event from Jesus' life that shows Him to be indeed the Christ, the Son of God (20:30). This theme of Jesus' perfect control over all things and all men continues through the events of the trials and crucifixion. Jesus tells Pilate, "You would have no authority over Me, unless it had been given you from above" (19:11).

It is important to John that we see that Jesus was not a helpless victim who was captured and put to death by His enemies, or even that He was a martyr; Jesus Christ willingly laid down His life for us. That His death was completely under His control—not man's—was confirmed by His resurrection (10:17-18). As we read of this scene of Jesus' arrest and of the soldiers falling helplessly to the ground we are reminded that in a coming day,

> *. . . At the name of Jesus every knee will bow, of those who are in heaven and on earth and under the earth, and that every tongue will confess that Jesus Christ is Lord, to the glory of God the Father. (Phil. 2:10-11)*

How blessed we are to have the opportunity to bow our knees *now* to this One that John's gospel has shown so clearly to be the Christ, the Son of God.

Leader's Notes

Study 1: The Word (John 1:1-18)

QUESTION 1

You will get a variety of answers. Try to tie each answer to a specific verse in the passage. You might ask one or more follow-up questions during your discussion of Question 1:

a. Why do you think John begins his gospel with "In the beginning . . . ," the same words that open the book of Genesis?

b. How do you reconcile these two statements from verse 1:

(1) "the Word was with God"

(2) "the Word was God"?

Attempts at explaining these statements appear in two interesting quotations in D. A. Carson, *The Gospel According to John, The Pillar New Testament Commentary* (Eerdmans, 1991), 117: "The 'Word does not by Himself make up the entire Godhead; nevertheless the divinity that belongs to the rest of the Godhead, belongs also to Him.' 'The Word was *with* God, God's eternal Fellow; the Word *was* God, God's own Self.'"

QUESTION 3

Some English translations use "comprehended" or "understood" in the second part of the verse. Others use "overcome." Emphasize to your group that both meanings of the word apply.

QUESTION 4

If time permits, look with your group at Matthew 3:1-12, Mark 1:4-8, and Luke 1:5-25 and 39-45 for more information about John the Baptist. Otherwise, you might just summarize this information.

QUESTION 8

The contrasts of the Mosaic Law with grace and truth and of Moses with Jesus Christ will be fairly obvious. John is contrasting the Old Testament order with the New Testament way. The Law defined God's standard for human righteousness. Grace and truth have always been among God's attributes, but Jesus came to embody those attributes and make them real to us. The basis for the relationship of sinful people to a holy God changes from condemnation under the Law to the opportunity for salvation by grace through faith. Don't let your group miss John's introduction of this new and gracious dealing of God with mankind.

Question 9

"The only begotten God" is a very literal rendering of the Greek *monogenes theos*. The term here translated "explained," "declared," or "made known" in the last phrase of verse 18 is literally to *exegete,* which means to "lay out in an orderly, analytical fashion."

Questions 10–12

These questions should generate wonderful lists of the great doctrinal truths of this passage. You might use them to summarize and pull together this lesson before discussing your group's responses to some of the personal application questions.

Questions 13–16

Personal application questions are often a way to make a weighty theological passage like this one more practical. However, the answers are sometimes, as the heading suggests, quite personal. Group members should not feel forced to share these answers. Questions 13–15 here should generate good sharing and discussion. Answers to question 16 might be too personal, particularly if this is your first week together as a group.

Study 2: The Messiah (John 4:1-42)

Question 2

To help your group members better understand the woman's surprise, remind them of who the Samaritans were. Second Kings tells us something of their early history. After the division of the Davidic kingdom, the northern ten tribes (termed in Scripture from then on as *Israel*, or *Samaria*, or *Ephraim*, in contrast to *Judah*, the southern kingdom) adopted an idolatrous worship of golden calves in place of the true worship of Jehovah at the temple in Jerusalem. Eventually God, as He had said He would, judged Israel by sending the Assyrians to defeat and capture them. The Assyrian policy for breaking up regional alliances and loyalties was to deport the populations of defeated countries to other places, so most of the Israelites were taken away and in their place other peoples were settled in the land. These strangers brought with them their own customs and religions. Over the centuries the remaining Israelites intermarried with these pagans, and the religion of Samaria became a mixture of pagan idolatry with a corrupted worship of Jehovah. Second Kings 17:41 summarizes the situation: they "feared the Lord and also served their idols."

By Jesus' time, the Samaritans had turned from idolatry and were following the teaching of Moses in the Pentateuch, although they rejected the rest of the Old Testament. For all these reasons, the Jews at the time of Christ viewed the Samaritans as an impure, unclean, mixed race with an equally mixed-up religion. The Samaritan woman at the well would have known all this, of course.

QUESTION 3

For a similar reaction, look back to John 2:47-50, the calling of Nathanael.

QUESTION 6

When the woman asks the men of Sychar, "This is not the Christ, is it?" (v. 29), she may not really be expressing doubt. She is perhaps being diplomatic, not wanting to offend by appearing to know more than those socially superior to her. She wants them to go to see for themselves.

QUESTION 7

In verses 31-33, Jesus presents principles of sowing and reaping: (1) the harvest is not far off, but now; (2) sowing and reaping are ongoing, and both are necessary to produce the harvest; (3) the reaper must not forget that he enjoys the fruit of the sower's labor.

QUESTION 9

The Jews would have thought of the Messiah as sent to the Jewish nation alone. Jesus, by revealing Himself as Messiah to the Samaritan woman, makes it clear that salvation and eternal life are offered freely to all. John is at great pains here in the early chapters of his gospel to make that clear.

QUESTION 10

These physical needs for rest and water clearly testify to Jesus' humanity even though the passage, and John's gospel as a whole, emphasize His deity.

QUESTION 11

Your group will quickly identify the three truths:

- God is spirit.
- Those who worship must do so "in spirit and truth."
- The Father seeks worshipers.

The phrase "in spirit and truth" may elicit good discussion as group members share their insights into its meaning.

Study 3: The Bread of Life (John 6:26-71)

QUESTION 1

Be sure your group sees from verse 27 that the Son of Man *gives* the "food which endures to eternal life." It is not earned, not even by faith.

QUESTION 2

God's way is always *believe* and *see,* not *see* and *believe*. They have seen Jesus Himself and yet have not believed (v. 36). Peter says, "We have believed and have come to know . . ." (v. 69). Faith comes first.

QUESTION 3

The crowd is probably implying that the miracle Jesus did the day before was something less than what Moses had done. The manna fed the Israelites in the wilderness for forty years and came, in their view, from heaven; the loaves and fish fed the multitude on the mountain just one meal and came, as far as they knew, from a boy's lunchbox.

The mention of the Prophet in verse 14 is likely a reference to Deuteronomy 18:15 and 18, where Moses warns the people against following the witchcraft and idolatry of the Canaanites and tells them of God's promise to raise up from among them a prophet like himself to lead them. Israel saw that promise partially fulfilled in all the prophets through the generations that spoke God's word to them. It is a promise, like so many others, that reaches its ultimate fulfillment in Jesus Christ.

QUESTION 7

All four phrases describe the same people. The Father gives and draws, but the individual must believe and appropriate Christ's sacrifice. There is perfect balance in God's plan between His sovereignty and man's responsibility.

QUESTION 8

Your group should be clear that Jesus is not speaking here about the Lord's Supper even though both the Bread of Life Discourse and the remembrance feast have to do with His death on the cross. Jesus would not celebrate the final Passover at which He instituted the symbols of remembrance (bread and wine) for another year.

QUESTIONS 10–12

These questions that center on the direct teaching about Christ and the Father could be used to help your group summarize and pull together truth from this long passage.

QUESTIONS 13–15

These three personal questions are intended for devotional self-examination; it may not be appropriate to share responses in your group. If you wish, rather than just skip these questions, you might rephrase them to ask in a general way what the possible answers might be. A discussion, for example, of ways that we may feed on Christ might be very helpful and instructive for some groups.

Study 4: The Eternal One (John 8:12-59)

QUESTION 1

"I am the Light of the world" is clearly a statement of Jesus' *deity* and *glory*, but it also holds other important implications:

- His *guidance* and *protection*. Since the Feast of Tabernacles was a commemoration of Israel's journey through the wilderness, Jesus' statement would recall the light of the pillar of fire.
- His work in *creation* (John 1:3-5).
- He is the *source of all human enlightenment* (John 1:4, 9).
- His presence in the world is *judgment* of it (John 3:17-21).

This statement, "I am the Light of the world," spoken as it was at the Feast of Tabernacles, paralleled the great lighting ceremonies of the feast. According to Jewish historians there were four great oil lamps set up in the Court of the Women, across from the Treasury. Accounts from the time say that these lamps lit the whole city of Jerusalem each night of the feast. There was much joyful singing and dancing associated with the lighting of the lamps.

QUESTION 3

"I am He." ("I am who I am" as God told Moses at the burning bush.) We must believe that He is God, that He is the self-existent One, the One who is changeless and eternally faithful.

Question 4

Your group should note in verses 28-29 the very clear statements of the essential oneness of the Father and the Son.

Question 5

Here we learn the kind of faith Jesus requires: faith that perseveres. Perseverance, commitment, and steadfast obedience prove that faith is genuine. The rewards are great: "You will know the truth, and the truth will make you free."

The opening of verse 31 presents a bit of a problem. Jesus seems to be teaching those who had believed (v. 30), but the argumentative tone exhibited in the accusations that follow (vv. 33-59) hardly seem consistent with people who believe. Either these were not truly committed believers or else there was a group of unbelievers standing nearby and challenging Him as He taught His new disciples.

Question 14

This question gets to the heart of the teaching presented in chapter 8, that Jesus did indeed claim to be fully God in every sense.

Verse 24: He is God, the only Savior and Redeemer of sinful men.

Verse 28: He is one with the Father in work, word, and will.

Verse 58: He is eternal, without beginning or end, and existed always in heaven before the incarnation.

Question 15

The oneness of the Father and Son is a constant theme in John's gospel and one of the great teachings of the book. Your group will enjoy discussing the truths about the Godhead seen in the listed verses as a way of consolidating the teaching of this chapter.

Questions 16 and 17

These questions are quite personal but might be worded more generally for the sake of discussion. Question 16 is an attempt to remind us all that "walking in the light" is also a day by day, decision by decision commitment to obedience to God's word (1 John 1:7;

Eph. 5:8). Similarly, question 17 asks us to appropriate individually the freedom from bondage to sin that is available to us through faith in Christ and obedience to His word.

Study 5: The Light of the World (John 9:1-41)

Question 2

It will be helpful to read aloud in your group session Matthew 5:14 and Ephesians 5:8-14. Emphasize to your group that although Jesus is no longer in the world physically, He is still in the world in the sense that His Spirit indwells believers; through them, His light still shines.

Question 4

Your group will probably find it interesting to notice the various responses to the blind man's healing.

- The neighbors seem uncertain that he is the same man as the blind beggar they have been accustomed to seeing. Perhaps they never really looked at him with any interest before now. By contrast, verse 1 tells us that Jesus, as He passed by, *saw* him.
- The Pharisees, of course, look for ways to discredit both this miracle and the One who has performed it. They question its timing (on the Sabbath); they question whether the man had really been blind; they refuse to accept the healed man's story; and finally they put him out of the synagogue.
- The parents are afraid and will attest to no more than the facts.
- The healed man shows remarkable confidence, even fearlessness, as he says, "If this man were not from God, He could do nothing." He chooses Jesus over the Jewish leaders even though as yet, he has never seen Him. He consistently acts in faith on the knowledge he has.

QUESTION 5

Jesus seeks him out and puts the question of faith to Him: "Do you believe in the Son of Man?" The man expresses his willingness to believe and Jesus reveals Himself to him. The man then believes and worships. Emphasize to your group that this is exactly the same progression we all follow when we put our faith in Him.

QUESTION 6

"Those who do not see" are people like the man born blind who recognize their need and are willing to accept the light that reveals the Savior. "Those who see" are people who think they are self-sufficient and who close their eyes against the light, as the Pharisees do here. The irony of verse 40 is overwhelming—they don't even know they have shut their eyes.

QUESTION 8

Your group may find several examples. These are some we should not miss:

- He is loving and gracious in correcting the disciples' mistaken ideas about assigning blame for the calamity of this man's physical blindness.
- The gift of sight to this blind beggar is an act of grace and compassion.
- The Lord takes the initiative. He sees the blind man that others fail to notice.
- The Lord seeks out the man after the Jewish leaders cut him off, saying in effect, "*They* won't have you, but I *will*."
- The Lord sees and loves the unnoticed and the outcasts.

QUESTION 9

From this chapter we see that "the works of God" include acts of compassion to relieve physical suffering as well as spiritual enlightenment. Whenever we see spiritual or physical healing, we see God at work. One other thought from verse 4 is that we as believers have "works of God" to do and a limited amount of time in which to do them (Eph. 2:10).

Study 6: The Good Shepherd (John 10:1-30)

Question 1

Note especially verse 3. The shepherd calls his sheep by name and leads them out. Jesus still calls us personally and individually. The shepherd leads his sheep rather than driving them. He as leader sets the pace, shows the way, and provides the example.

Question 2

Jesus is saying that He is the way through which each of His sheep must receive eternal life and enter into relationship with God. The picture of Jesus as the "door," though, probably includes more than just entering into salvation through Him, since He says in verse 11 that the sheep will "go in and out and find pasture." The thought here of "he will be saved" would seem to include the idea of being kept safe by the watchful shepherd. The sheep enjoy the perfect balance of being led out to pasture to feed when it is safe to do so and being brought into the fold when danger threatens. The sheep enjoy both liberty and security, provision and protection, because Jesus is "the door of the sheep."

Question 3

The thieves and robbers are identified here by what they do. They do not enter by the door; the sheep do not recognize their voices; and they come to steal, kill, and destroy. In the context here Jesus seems to refer to the Jewish leaders who do not accept His message. We have seen them in action in chapter 9. They tried repeatedly to destroy the credibility of the formerly blind man's testimony and ended by excommunicating him from the synagogue. They have evidenced their true motives and their lack of concern for the well-being of the sheep.

QUESTION 5

Again, the hired hand may be best identified by what he does. He does not protect the sheep but runs away when trouble comes. Note that, like the thieves and robbers, the hired hand does not care for the sheep but seeks only his own gain.

QUESTION 6

Verse 16 is an important one, especially for those of us who are Gentiles. Jesus uses this opportunity to say that He, as the Good Shepherd, has other sheep not of the sheepfold of Judaism. We notice that both groups, Jewish and Gentile believers, will be part of one flock. The verb tenses are interesting. The other sheep "*will hear* [His] voice" in the future, but He says, "I *have* other sheep." They already belong to Him.

QUESTION 9

John 10:27-30 is one of the great passages that teach the eternal security of the believer. Be sure you make time to read these important verses with your group, emphasizing that security rests not on our hold on the Lord but on His hold on us.

QUESTION 10

The "great Shepherd" of Hebrews 13 is the risen Lord through whom God equips us in every good thing to do His will. The "Chief Shepherd" of 1 Peter 5 will return to reward faithful service to Him (in this passage, the service of faithful church elders).

QUESTION 12

Psalm 23 looks at the shepherd/sheep relationship from the point of view of the sheep. It shows how all the promises of the Good Shepherd in John 10 work out in the practical experience of one of His sheep. A discussion of the parallels in these two Scripture passages might be a good way to close today's group time. An alternative, of course, would be sharing from the personal application question (question 13).

Study 7: The Resurrection and the Life (John 11:1-46)

QUESTION 2

Like the blind man's congenital condition, Lazarus's illness had the purpose of ultimately bringing glory to God and to His Son. We can learn from these incidents that handicaps, illness, and even death may have a good purpose far beyond what our earthly eyes may see. To discern such a purpose in human suffering requires that we see them from a point of view that is eternal, not just earthly or temporal.

QUESTION 4

Sleep as a term for death is not just a euphemism. The New Testament writers convey their attitude toward the physical death of believers as they use this word "sleep" to remind us that death is neither final nor irreversible. Physical death for the believer is not like death for an unbeliever. For the unbeliever it is the first step of the eternal death that is the punishment for his sin. The believer's body awaits the resurrection to eternal life.

QUESTION 5

Martha understands Jesus' statement for what it is, a proclamation of His deity. Her responding confession of faith in verse 27 makes this clear.

QUESTION 6

John seems to invite this comparison as he gives details about the stone at the entrance to each of the tombs and the grave clothes in each case. Jesus gave Lazarus his earthly life back, reversing the processes of physical decay and reuniting his soul and spirit with his body. However, Lazarus was still in a mortal body that would die a second time.

Jesus' body, after He was raised, was a new kind of body. It was not impeded by physical barriers, for example, although it was a physical body. (Thomas was invited to touch the wounds, and Jesus ate with His disciples.) After His resurrection Jesus had a body that was no longer mortal, no longer subject to death. You might reread 1 Corinthians 15:20. Jesus was the first one to receive this kind of body, which all believers will receive when He returns.

Study 8: The Way, the Truth, and the Life (John 14:1-31)

Question 2

These verses give us very little in the way of a physical description of the Father's house. What Jesus emphasizes to His disciples is that it is a home for believers with the Father and the Son. The important thing is that we shall be with Him, not what the place is like. Your group should notice also that it is a place prepared by the Lord Himself, that there are many rooms, with a place for every believer, and that Jesus here promises to return to take believers to be with Him.

Question 3

He is the way; Jesus does not just *show* us the way. Faith in Him—that He is who He said He was, God in the flesh—and faith in His atonement for our sins constitute the only way to the Father's house. He says here, "No one comes to the Father but through Me." Our pluralistic, relativistic world finds this exclusivity most offensive, but there is no doubt that it is what the Scripture teaches.

Question 4

He is the truth. The verses in parentheses from the book of John remind the reader of Jesus' previous claims to truth and thus to deity. Because He is God, He is truth—eternal verity, reality, the right viewpoint on everything. The references to the "true bread" and the "true vine" remind us that He is also the fulfillment of the Old Testament shadows and types.

QUESTION 5

He is the life. Eternal, spiritual life is probably what is primarily in view here, although one cannot help but remember the references in John 1 to the Son's role in the creation of earthly, physical life as well. Another aspect that should be discussed is the abundant life mentioned in John 10:10. The life to be found in the Lord Jesus is not just everlasting; it is a different quality of life that is even for here and now because it includes that dimension of a spirit alive to God which we lack without Him.

QUESTION 6

The promises about prayer are in the context of serving Christ, of doing works for Him, to spread the message of the gospel. He says the disciples will do greater works than the ones they have seen Him do. Many scholars take this statement to mean greater in the sense of farther reaching: the apostles carried the message all over the known world in the years following Jesus' death and resurrection. In that sense, they had a much broader impact than Jesus alone had had in the three years of His earthly ministry.

This access to the Father in prayer, and the answers that we are promised, are based on the unity of the Father and the Son in will and purpose.

Study 9: The Vine (John 15:1-16)

QUESTION 1

True here has the same meaning it does in John 6 when Jesus speaks of Himself as the "true bread" that came down from heaven. The manna was a *type*, a *figure*, a *shadow* in the Old Testament Scriptures. The passages in Psalm 80 and Isaiah 5 present Israel as God's vine, a vine that has failed to produce good fruit even though the Lord has done everything for it. Jesus here presents Himself as the true (faithful, real) vine, the One that will produce good fruit that will glorify the Father.

QUESTION 2

The relationship is one of such intimacy that it is like the branches which live (abide, remain, dwell) in Christ the vine. The Father tends this relationship by pruning or cleaning the branches. Verse 3 reminds us that the cleansing is through the written Word of God. The goal is fruit. The branch is not just to draw life from the vine to sustain itself, but to produce something good for the vinedresser, God the Father. Christian character is described as fruit in Galatians 5:22-23. In addition, souls won for Christ may be considered fruit, which seems to be what is in mind in John 15:16.

QUESTIONS 3 & 5

You may want to consult reliable commentaries on these questions. You will find several interpretations of verses 2 and 6. The verses included in question 3 are some that your group may find useful for discussion. This is one of the Bible passages about which it is easier to say what it does *not* mean than what it does. Emphasize to your group that the branches which do not bear fruit or do not abide cannot be believers who have lost their salvation. That interpretation is in direct contradiction to too many other Scriptures, e.g., John 10:27-28. Otherwise, there seem to be three fairly common interpretations:

1. These are believers who are not obeying and serving and have been physically disciplined—taken home to heaven—as in 1 Corinthians 11:30-32.

2. The people in verse 2 are "branches in Me," and thus true believers whom the Lord "lifts up" so that they may bear fruit. "Lifts up" is another way the Greek word translated "takes away" can be understood. However the people in verse 6 who "do not abide in [Him]" are counterfeit Christians, like Judas, who were never really abiding in the vine, but just appeared to be.

3. The people referred to in verses 2 and 6 are counterfeits in both cases. These are people who appear to be Christians but are shown not to be because they have no fruit in their lives for God. Again Judas is a prime example. See also Matthew 7:15-20, John 6:66, or 1 John 2:19.

Question 9

The important thing to note here is that Jesus' love for His own is active. He does not merely *say* He loves; in this passage we see that He makes them His friends (v. 15), He makes the Father's words known to them (v. 15), and He has chosen them for His service (v. 16). Most significantly of all, He will soon "lay down his life for his friends" (v. 13).

Study 10: The One in Control (John 18:1-11)

Question 2

A Roman cohort could comprise as many as six hundred men, but calling this a "cohort" would not necessarily mean all six hundred were present. The soldiers came with lanterns, torches, and weapons. Apparently they anticipated having to search the mountainside at night for Jesus, and they expected resistance. There were crowds of people in Jerusalem for Passover, and Jesus was a popular figure. John is the only one of the gospel writers to tell us that the Romans were involved in the arrest.

Question 7

Peter's actions here are completely consistent with what we have seen of him up until this point. He has said he will lay down his life for the Lord (13:37). Cutting off the servant's ear is his rather clumsy effort to protect Jesus, as he was probably intending to cut off the man's head. He is loyal and courageous, but rash and impetuous. He acts before thinking things through.

Question 8

As we see from the referenced passages, the cup is the cup of suffering, but it is also the symbol of God's will and plan. By contrast here, the sword becomes the symbol of man's way, the way of human effort and strength. Ultimately it is the symbol of man's rebellion against the will of God. Jesus takes the cup the Father has given Him, but Peter takes up the sword of rebellion against the will of God.

Question 9

Your group will have a variety of items on their lists. They will probably include some or all of these:

- Jesus is where He can easily be found.
- Jesus goes out to them. He has been waiting for them to come (Mark 14:41-43).
- He speaks first, asking, "Whom do you seek?"
- They fall back when He says, "I am He."
- He protects His disciples (John 17:12).
- He tells Peter to put away the sword.
- He heals Malchus's ear.
- He knows exactly what is happening, and submits to it: "The cup which the Father has given Me, shall I not drink it?"

Question 10

Walking on the water to the disciples as they struggle to control their boat in the storm shows Jesus' complete control over the forces of nature. In John 18 we see His control over human beings.

Question 14

This question is an effort to help us moderate our tendency to criticize Peter. He was strong and brave; he loved Jesus very much. His failures recounted in this chapter warn us that if Peter could fail so utterly, anyone can. Possible lessons might be any of the following:

- Beware human confidence.
- We cannot follow the Lord in our own strength.
- Denial comes easily; standing up is hard.
- We are, by our nature, inconsistent—attacking with the sword one minute, denying Jesus entirely the next.